Vahni Capildeo

Dark & Unaccustomed Words

egg box

Dark & Unaccustomed Words

First Published, 2011, by Egg Box Publishing
www.eggboxpublishing.com

Book Design:
Nathan Hamilton
& Su Yen Pang

Printed and bound by:
MPG Biddles, Kings Lynn
www.biddles.co.uk

ISBN: 978-0956928917

egg box

Dark & Unaccustomed Words

by Vahni Capildeo

for Nicholas Laughlin

By The Same Author

No Traveller Returns (Salt, 2003)
Person Animal Figure (Landfill, 2005)
Undraining Sea (Egg Box, 2009)

CONTENTS

FRAMBOYÁN 11
THE PALE BEAST / LA BLANCHE BICHE 12
THE DRIVING LESSON: I. 13
THE DRIVING LESSON: II. 14
TREE WITH A SILVER LINING 15
ALMOND, BEARDED 16
EVEN IN SLEEP, REFRAINING 17
MOVING AND MOVED 18
GETTING RID OF THOMAS 19
PAST INHABITANT 20
GIVE ME MORE TIME, SAID NIGHT 22
ABOUT 23
JOURNAL OF ORDINARY DAYS 25
METAMORPHOSES 29
SAHARA DREAM CUBES 34
CALLS 35
AS IN THE SUNLIGHT AND GIVEN HUMAN
FORM IT IS LESS USUALLY IMPOSSIBLE TO
BE SUBJECT TO THE MINUTIÆ OF WARMTH 36
TEMPERATURE CONTROLLED ENVIRONMENT 37
GO FIGURE! 39
FOR ADJECTIVES ARE ONE ROAD CUT INTO
THE PRECIPICE BORDERING PERFECTION 40
TO A FLUTE, CONTINUOUS
(AND THE PARTICULAR SWEETNESS) 41
THE SALAMANDER IS SO COLD 42
MORE SOLID FIRE 43
SINKING LIGHTWELLS 44
CALL IT SIMPLE: TWO EXTERIORS 45
180° EEYLOPS 46
WE'RE PROCEEDING, WEIGHTED FOR SWIFTNESS 47
OXIDANTS 48

CONTENTS

AFTER THE EXPLOSION 49
THE ROUND POND 50
THOUGHTS OF THE DEAD 52
VACANT POSSESSION 54
JOURNAL OF A FAIR SIZED CITY 55
MY HIPPEASTRUMS AND MYSELF 57
COMPLETELY F****D 58
OUTSIDE 59
THE VEGETABLES OF CONTEMPT 60
BOLDFACED 61
DON JUAN DE QUETZALCOATL 62
OUR LADY OF STOKE NEWINGTON 63
THANKSGIVING THANK-YOU NOTE 64
JOYFUL, TOWARDS A WEDDING DAY 65
THE NINTH DUCK IS CROSSING THE WATER 66
TEJ JASPAL AND HIS TOOTH 67
YOU HAVE YOUR SPACE 68
THE CARIBBEAN EDITOR IMAGINES
EARTHQUAKES 69
ON NOT WRITING AS A WEST INDIAN WOMAN 71
AMONG 72
OBJECTION POETRY 73
GROSS PIPEWORK, SUBTLE MUSIC 74
ABOUT THE SHAPE OF THINGS 75
ABOUT THE BRIGHTNESS OF THINGS 76
THE SERENITY 77
BREATHE AGAIN 78
VOWEL POEM: ALBEDO 79

But generally the high stile is disgraced and made foolish and ridiculous by all wordes affected, counterfait, and puffed vp, as it were a windball carrying more countenance than matter, and can not be better resembled then to these midsomer pageants in London, where to make the people wonder are set forth great and vglie Gyants marching as if they were aliue, and armed at all points, but within they are stuffed full of browne paper and tow, which the shrewd boyes undverpeering, do guilefully discouer and turne to a great derision: also all darke and vnaccustomed wordes, or rusticall and homely, and sentences that hold too much of the mery & light, or infamous & vnshamefast are to be accounted of the same sort, for such speaches become not Princes, nor great estates, nor them that write of their doings to vtter or report and intermingle with the graue and weightie matters.

George Puttenham,
'Of the high, low, and meane subiect',
in *The Arte of Poesie* (1589)

The fisherman will set his tray of hooks
and ease them one by one into the flood.
His net of twine will strain the liquid billow
and take the silver fishes from the deep.
But my own hand I dare not plunge too far
lest only sand and shells I bring to air
lest only bones I resurrect to light.

Martin Carter,
'Till I Collect',
in *Poems of Resistance* (1954)

'Fayre damesel,' seyde Sir Launcelot, 'know y[e] in this contrey ony adventures nere hande?'

'Sir knyght,' seyde the damesel, 'here ar adventures nyghe, and thou durst preve hem.'

'Why sholde I not preve?' seyde sir Launcelot. 'For for that cause com I hydir.'

Thomas Malory,
'A Noble Tale of Sir Launcelot du Lake',
in *Works*, ed. by Eugène Vinaver, second edn (1971)

DARK & UNACCUSTOMED WORDS

FRAMBOYÁN

For Deana Rankin

That trees had evolved to eat other trees.
That this happened at the end of a garden.
That this was first noticed in a small tree's wincing.
That the larger tree was bending in, whipped by no wind,
a flamboyant tree and not in flower, bunched to a beak.
Dwarf and royal poinciana trees: almost one kind:
at the end of a Trinidad childhood garden.

That the small tree visibly respired; menaced,
yet stock still, spread and ruffled, animal
yet green; this one yes in flower as if on fire
yet in devouring distress letting air in
yet – feather-tipped and all aflame – just like an offshoot
of what stood over.

Hardly leafed, intent and purposeful,
stacked altostratus storm-bark discovering its due
moved in to take, concave against odds of weather.

Pitiless, we witness small uprootings; turn,
with each untreelike recommencing; retreat
further into the house, feel ourselves delicate;
stridently walk, shuddering bolts shut, instinct outraged,
know: we are next, who shall be due to fall under green shade.

But lock the doors (the well-made doors: investments, property).
The thing is busy outside (that tree evolved to eat
other trees). It is good our doors are good.

And indeed it centred in – the earth; the slate; the concrete –
And indeed it entered wading. For our doors were wood.

THE PALE BEAST / LA BLANCHE BICHE

Inside a green and leafy wood
twigs snap, sap-sharp scents rise.
How shall I have recourse from this?
There is no leaf-green wood nearby
but one kept under lock and key.

I am a white-bloused girl by day,
nights a pale and fleeing beast.
In crying silence all give chase.
And she who gave me birth
of all of them the worst.

Go call them off, who'll call them off,
who'll find, affrighted from my skin,
what were girl's breasts? Fine guests.
Set to. That is my flesh within
the dish you banquet on.

THE DRIVING LESSON: I.

He asked for slow ladies, but he wanted snow ladies.
I responded positively –

> Knowing that you were somewhere in the city centre,
> and that, whatever the event, finding you is restful –
> Magnolia snow done its drift, white petals melting pink
> brownwards towards the pigeon ground, your new usual drink
> fresh valencianas in the Anglo-Saxon nook.
> Unnatural blaze these summer days. Shade's a waiting book
> over your hand under your face, restive where it could
> pace away as print keeps doing, in memory of whole worlds.

And he asked again, "Are you the slow lady?"
You know that I said "Yes."

> My, he looked pleased, tried to focus. I looked at his eyes.
> They fetched no distance. Didn't traffic in light. Disguise
> was a stranger to them, just about as much use
> as a burglar whose house of choice, broken into, shows
> equally empty of personality, possessions.
> Journal grey giving way to ridged silver horizons,
> to a coin sellotaped to the base of a pint glass,
> glimpsed only in draining seconds, foam over iris.

Well strapped into the learner driver's seat,
shoulders kerbwards, looking left, looking right,
I receive a stinging blow to the wrist.
He says that's been the best lesson yet.

He asked for slow ladies, but he wanted snow ladies.

I get out. Walk to the park.

THE DRIVING LESSON: II.

People like those you said were friends are waiting in the square.
Some not alive, all attentive. For each one, a tree.
The sharp-witted one straight in front of lilac leaves,
her henna head a streetlight contrast. None is too grave.
We are concentrating – not on speech, which is Translation,
and ah how fluently is spoken Translation's speech! –
a sense of community we're concentrating on,
quiet glad as of news of birth brought to chairs of death.
I feel myself keep away. Flinch from flinching. Stiller
than those, not alive, who cannot prevent the rustle
of involuntary movement, helpful and ignored.
One tree in especial, its purple overshadow,
brings such horror of the vigil to me, I look up.
Seeing more exactly our fellows' situation –
I believe I mean the trees – will bring the secret words
into ear, into heart, earth them up, understanding
alike, and growing in likeness. – Oh what are these
up there? Fingernails, crabbed and pearlescent, canopied
fingernails, irreducible. Whose leaves will they be?

TREE WITH A SILVER LINING

i.m. the dead and living of Hiroshima and Nagasaki

Above the fence the silver underside of leaves
several stems next door to make one slender tree
do not ascribe distress   or a wish for peace
neither inanimate nor animate
the movement of the wind the movement of the tree

it is a human thing to think the leaf is green
silver side up   each leaf fled   deflecting heat
leaves leaving the holder of the thought of tree
how thin this leaf is   wind-tossed   seen like that
the shadows on the fence have more heft, in their way

branched shadows on the fence outweigh the slender tree
black leaves bunched like fruit   like excavation finds
like trowels   like the speaking clock   like relief
where and wherever leaves change   never far
the fear   the flash that stamped apart shadow and leaf.

Come home, soon and quickly, love. The butterfly tree,
light on the fence, slender stems, make thoughts in me,
if you arrive late, you will find me away,
neither of here nor of now; do not leave,
do not leave believing bereavement, who can stay?

ALMOND, BEARDED

The tree could not believe how it became involved
with her, a human being born to the disease –
short-timed, hyper-mobile – common to her kind,
their swift-fallen alertness, bright desire to unpiece.

Years it had taken growing to produce a crotch,
a midway knot of outward shadow, marking in
the start of rift the one support for both upflung
branches (what she too easily called arms). Oh, last –

Dim it evolved mythologies, two-memoried
to hedge her gently (unable breather skywards,
rose and yearning mist), maybe for true remembered
a wave-borne destroying, more height than canopy.

Not think out evil yet join her in grieving over
earthquakes not withstood, the upturned white plaza,
sea's incursions far inland reaping the least of twigs.

It too could love now, unrenewably, reward
love because unrenewable –
Sudden and level in eventual dissolving,
mortal and tree.

EVEN IN SLEEP, REFRAINING

When I heard the sad adulterers Tristan and Iseult
had placed a sword between them as they slept, so to avoid
sexual congress in the forest, my first and filthy thought:
how much you can do despite a sword, lean above maybe,
long soothes down flanks whose fighting muscles bunch and do not rest,
waterfalls of pitiful caresses run misplaced.
But those two know swords, the humiliations of wound care,
instantaneous gross damage. Cousins to that-which-broke.
One blade, lying coldly, puts a guard upon the mind,
trains body, motive, separate in the forest of their want.
Sharp metal cuts unmoved upon the first unconscious move,
prevents love reaching through their sleep, or sleeping hand in hand.

MOVING AND MOVED

They are keeping us apart: cloud from dazzle;
mirror from window; oboe from embouchure;
dusk – dawn – to the abolition of pianos.
For they are jealous as mortals can be, once
one god's on the move; want to know where to point
when seeking in abyssal need a pointer
telling them: *the blue sky is friendly, and yours.*
You turtle-turn your backs, bow heads, clench shoulders,
walk away without one look up? Your resource
is still there still caring whether you go singing.
One god to point to. Not more than one.
Keeping
one god apart from another, how easy
can that be, given the spheres of influence
move according to acts of worship? Who would
joke with one god, joke about no god, works to
keep gods apart.
It is not for fear lest deities
turn their backs and walk off into marriage or
deeper, more trenchant inscrutability.
It is so a handful of mud, a handful
of water, remains enough to make them laugh.
With us.

GETTING RID OF THOMAS
For McMahon

The man said to do it
so we went to find him
and he was cursing us
   I'm tired of what's happening
   to green lands that I love
His voice made me more tired
   I heard, as I struck him,
   something helmeted roar
I swear to you, my head
was bare, I was prepared,
I knew I was entering church.

My friend from stony lands
FitzUrse, you changed your name
   I only have her voice…

FitzUrse, de Morville, de Tracy and le Breton (de Brito) slew Thomas a Becket at Canterbury. FitzUrse ('son of a bear', Norman) has a legendary connexion with the McMahon ('son of a bear', Irish) clan.

PAST INHABITANT

For Emma Dillon

Even if it was your white sleeve rising through the earth under woods you'd not care for, weak cultivars, modern beyond use for your time – even if you raised your sleeved arm, reassuring, I understood now as if it were yesterday and no quarry, as if gravel did not spit in the face of search for unreconstitutable wings, unrecorded weddings, house unimprinted, drained of traitors. Laughter leaves no shadow, rushing for refuge in the honeycombs, storage caverns collapsed, stream wiped, the action of mercy and chalk.

Douce amie, you, meanwhile, walking tall between much taller hedges, counted, in another garden, the singing of birds, the young ones (especially starlings) needing what you figured as a window for the slow illuminations of their induction into song. Numbers of them, flung from the nest into nests not their own, dimwits, interjecting wrong notes or twists. Ignorant what makes melody – How to vary, still, shake, depart, fuse the necessary signal for two needs: love and territory. Entreaty and repulsion. How hard they sing! Elaborate necessity defeats itself, reaving sung from song: starlings plummet, falling from branches, sometimes dying. Come. Go. Carried away.

A henge of good intentions a megalith of effort uphill of slippage perpetual uphill with no downhill thought grinding thought tooth upon tooth so much strength surely for giving forehead wrenched to the incline set to an identical angle as once the nick-in-the-neck stone that old straight track for not seeing for not looking from desired to required from excruciating to crossed. Send out a call for bonfires. Give no warning against burning. Make a blaze of every gradient.
Our ships are coming in.

> I wished for this in the valley where
> the lake stays an oblong below
> the ridge that turns back the harsher winds
> where leaves from our apple trees blew.

I looked from the window to the well.
You stepped up almost to the door.
You stood, unawares, among your men.
I stepped down, walked into this song.

I brought my life back into the house
of stone, brown and white as the cloth
that slipped kindly under brown-white earth.
I rise now, returning by choice.

GIVE ME MORE TIME, SAID NIGHT

For Barbara Graziosi

. . . but you're setting me to teach
how suns build up into compendiums:
one,
one,
one to the power of zero?

Given I hold more light,
give me more time, said night;
you will not miss day.
Time enough – so much must reach
you, summing, bright as ever:
each slowly travelling star
seems,
beaming,
blink-like, desperate.
Look! No day's my comparate.
This needs time: that goes far:
wait, a whole work, like heaven.

And radiant intersections give up sight.

Drop day.

Admit I hold more light.

ABOUT

For Pat Bishop

Aware of these rooms five four three two one hundred years old all about us for hundreds of people each year and none not one room for us this night feels the blocks waiting three two one the rooms have emptied out and each is bored by its own pulse the core of blackness that is the waiting of interested stone for there has been nothing like this for them nothing like us except once twice perhaps each century. Sssh, everybody's here.

"We have come to the place of which I told you . . ."

> Hills set on gulf, surf set on hill, rift city –
> In the skin of a house a hissy fit,
> a crying jag, it veins thermometers,
> gradual because quick-pressed, desiccative,
> scales over eyes the exit fangs first?
> Snakeform's a total way, rice-paper slough
> shines of got out sun-bitten rolled between
> a rough place and somewhere much like this.

"Some birds line their nests with snakeskin."

> Rare things do happen occasionally
> (remorse, the true dream, a dead one's call?) –
> the all-purpose assailant's face turned helpful,
> the knife-strapped taxi driver touching wires
> to start a car shot to cobwebs. And you fail:
> it's that your appointment's with extreme cases,
> solids alight by millions, cellular,
> disranking every day all too much rarity.

"You can't go back to a piece of dusting
and reflect upon it."

> This time she's brought some handouts on panic,
> pink sheets (the chair kicked from beneath a plan,

what feels like permanent fatal errors) –
consisting as they do of eminently
sayable, beautiful effective sounds,
what transfers into poems? Enough recall
one voice? Listen. Language dreams about this:
the infant making bird-soft divisions of dawn.

". . . could just be dot dot dot."

At night, you see, there seems to be one lit room. Who is at its exit, in the doorway, back turned? The soft rectangle of human frame widens. Who waits within the metal edging? In this state of nervousness, forearms go cold seconds before hands catch fire, excessive lotuses of flame. Would you – two dark torches loose at your sides – would you walk into the first of the long dark corridors in a building that consists more nearly of corridors than any that should ever have been designed? Each corridor runs like a spill of milk on a black tile reflected in a smoked glass ceiling clapped on the width of one layer of a hotel. These corridors are dark; you would feel them all like paleness? Though there were light I could not name their handcrafted nougat colours, gentler, intentionally washed-out. I walk in the dark, and you feel the walls' paleness? For we ourselves are luminous. Except we do not give off light.

JOURNAL OF ORDINARY DAYS

For Ron Paste

I.

Do I look like the sort of person who's not fit
to go out and buy a pen on her own? The phrase
"May I borrow a biro" is unspeakable
for its vocalic ugliness. The task in hand,
this third daze of work, is dis- and rearranging,
suspecting, assessing, keying in and tagging
all the historical spellings of the verb QUIT.
"That can't be a lot? QUIT is such a little verb?"
But people have been quitting for centuries, and
especially in Scotland, all in different ways.
So this third daze I break from work to buy a pen.
Let it be an ethical biro. I set out
for the fair trade Quaker shop. The assistants talk
more than I do, showing me pens two fingers thick
encrusted like scary rhinestoneri charging
pink-purple, delivering jabs in the eye
to mass-produced-capitalist-consumerist-
conformity. But not suitable to be housed
in the zoo of QUIT. Sorry, silent, cash intact,
I look elsewhere, and not far off the ordinary
rewards this initiative: sell-it-all, old-fashioned,
like nineteen fifty-three, nearly customer-free,
a newsagent of the English variety.
The cardboard cradles for goods on these shelves wouldn't
aspire to store shoes, let alone to be reborn
as cut-out stars for a wonky schoolhouse mobile.
With reverence for age, I abstract a biro
not quite dried up. I softfoot over to the queue.
So form a line of one, outnumbered by cashiers.
The older assistant keeps things under control.
But can't seem to stop his helper singing singing
singing to him lovingly in a high-pitched tone,
"I'm going to put you in chains and take you home.

I'm going to put you in chains and take you home."
Neither raises his voice; nor does the one quiet down.
In a queue of one I shall queue, change in hand, wait,
queue in a queue of one, however long it takes.
Anything is better than going back to QUIT.
I can buy a pen on my own. I'm fit.

II.

We are not born with an instinctive understanding of the mangrove.
We drove out and booked and paid to step in the flat boat bound for
mangrove.
It feeds on land dissolved ocean dismissed sunset deferred, the mangrove.
Snakes up top stayed squamous yellow knots of sleep guides tried in vain
to shake awake,
the silky anteater too knotted in sleep on high.
The mangrove the movement of the mangrove.
Look lively.

Like the ribbing of a gothic cathedral inlaid with no stone,
inlay of scuttling tree crabs, branch-attached above-ground oysters,
sprung
inlay as if pollution resides not in the invisible hills,
inlay of wickerwork red and spotted white and black by nature growing
not green
what is this mangrove, salt-nourished, where sea floods inlets?
Can we breathe here?

Yes and in yogic and Carib perfection
the swaying incarceration over
still and suddenly all into blue
perfection of lake and fluorescent ibis
winging to roost in perfection of dusk.
Will this or any memory of serenity
permeate his sleep – your two-year-old
who's slumbered now beside us in the boat
long since we stepped apart from automotive dust?
Once or twice he woke and looked.
Will peace keep with him?

III.

My darling love, as evening falls
and for the first time I breathe air
without the fine and germy plume
that sweeps and moults from vent to chair,
I feel the freshness that derives
from parking lots that run beside
rivers diverted underground
and cold-pressed tourists who deride
how like a driven hog I streak
back to my filthy pen. I glow
like tea-lights in a scented tub
at your approach. The dark I know.

IV.

You, detesting lizards but having been given,
years ago, a rubber shark plus half a diver,
are insulated from this lunchroom shock: riven,
his arm, the croc engrossing, jaws that devour.
What is the ground over which newspapers murmur?
Unimaginable, unimaginable.
Aren't there shark bites so sharp that what makes the surface
is gamely swimming torso, red pennants engulfed?
Unimaginable, unimaginable.
What breaks the surface –
Maybe gratitude for cold climates and dry land.
A sense of detachment from that which moves the hand.

V.

Sometimes I dream in a language that is mine only by scratches,
but I can get the tune of it, a whole conversation
between strangers friendly to each other, dawdling behind me
somewhere outdoors, a sandy cone of syllables
rising and falling, whole sentences
coming smattering to the surface from an occluded source.

Sometimes it is the actual people around me on a journey
whose language drifts into another throughout my dreams,
the prerequisite for transformation always being
that both tunes already are familiar to my memory,
so that the Irish have become Jamaican; the Spanish, Trinidadian;
while the French stay French, but sound maternal, a loving thirty-nine.

Some time ago, I dreamt that I could no longer see by means of light.
Without knowing by experience, or even scientifically,
what this would involve, I saw by means of heat.
How gradually I registered the changeable reddish-dark,
and that my dream environment was room-like, and enclosure,
and that the pulsing blue was situated in someone, not unlike
yourself, whose breathing seemed too loud to me
because of the lack of light; and how, instead of speaking,
you comforted my shoulder, both incandescing white.

METAMORPHOSES

For Liz Irwin

A palm tree sprang up just within the gate to the park. Nobody would remove it; the park was not due for refurbishment for another three and a half months. It was not the kind of palm tree that anyone would normally try to grow in England's climate, though it was not impossible that a palm tree of this variety could survive even the so-called severer winters in the 'Home Counties'. However, it was growing abnormally fast for a palm tree of any variety in any climate. Having started off like the green ridged dorsal fin of an earth fish sticking up through the soil, it now presented a solid stump covered with a furze of thorns. The crown of the palm was several-fronded and not soft. It grew fast but was not equal to the head height of most of the adult local residents. The freak tree continued to look the same, but taller day by day.

A crowd of people near the church down the road was discussing whether the palm tree really was of the variety that the person who spent a lot of time abroad and sometimes gave lectures in the community hall had identified it as, and whether it should be removed or protected. Distilling palm liquor was not an option. It could not be tapped for gum – it did not seem like a source of aromatic resin. It had grown fast but borne no fruit. Its shade was less than a clock hand, dependent on the sometimeish English sun.

As I do not go to church and was only passing alongside the friendly group, I heard some of their discussion but cannot report what they concluded. "Why don't you write about that?" these friends called out, meaning the tree at the end of the road. But I did not want to write about it.

It stayed.

One day a strange bird roosted in it, but before anyone could decide whether the wild thing should be culled as a harbinger of disease, it had flown away, leaving one feather that somebody who was not local picked up, took away, and never mentioned or displayed. I think he had connections in the fire service.

"Butterflies in your stomach?"
"No. Moths."
"All the kinds of moth there are?"
"Perhaps . . . no. Neither the death's-head moths from another sinister story felt not seen, nor the moths of memory, silver-gold thumbprints in low gear about the managing of candles when electricity failed on dark afternoons of the Rainy Season in happy third-world households where constant novelty held children unafraid."
"These moths of the oesophagus are the widest-winged."
"They are denser than cocoa pods stamped by lifelong illiterate chocolate producers on the Gold Coast."
"That may be a short *lifelong*, yet little living's all bitter."
"The insides are in a flap over these moths."
"Do they go high or from side to side? Do they line up wedges in profusion?"
"They do not register as moths. They would outweigh bats."
These moths work together to turn over and over the blood-supplied slab known as stomach. Only gradually does the idea of moth lodge itself in the worried mind seeking internal confirmation.

The soft skin around those eyes was an imagined area. Its fascination was colour and shadow played at blending. The skin itself a non-entity since correct application procedure had been followed, the sparkle of expression was a figment of the pigment. They might have been doll eyes. The author of such smugness found the smugness an irritant like the sun that fetches out lounger people in the business of self-protection from rays it is a choice to bask in.

Please disregard the silver oblong that is not a screen. If your upbringing and the predetermined imaginings intended to supplement but now displacing mind find it easier to ignore the source diffusing light by terming it a screen, feel free to do so as it would be a significant mistake for anyone to attempt to behave towards it as s/he might towards a window in an enclosed space not primarily designed for comfort – not secured, nor certainly supervised. Try to ensure that you do not turn your back to the 'screen' or look directly at it, and maintain some distance while keeping it to the right of you. Please also disregard the reclaimed pedestal-mounted stone basin. What is not a window is intended to light this, which is not a sink. On the black paper floating there, black words are being written. If the almost automatic pen point is distracted, it will punch through the paper. There will be a flare of silver. Your hands will be freezeburnt off the paper as you find yourself standing before the font. The mistake will retort through the bone between the eyes. They will think that is you, although both sides will have gone cold.

The polished obsidian floor was made without a budget. As in the memory of a privileged child whose family holidays were partly spent waiting in banks used by money launderers and laid out on Temple-of-the-Sun proportions (one- and three-way glass sealing the dealing in bonds, james bonds), the artificiality of the lighting implies that whatever does not explain itself is nonetheless spared from presenting its perfectly possible explanations.

You see from the angle of a fly on a wall so shiny as to be insupportable to insect feet. You can see everything and you can see in the dark and you've switched nothing on, nor is your head helmeted with a vision-enhancer.

Who is that in a block of wood? Who would use a six-by-four-by-three-foot natural pencil: a block of wood the size of a person's coffin, and not a coffin or any other kind of wooden form? Would you wield it to write to her when you can't bear to have the answers?

May it remain a block, and eyeless?

That's a whistle. A beam of air has pared a strip of wood from the block's hip. Shrilling again, the ethereal surgery: it shrills till your flesh clings on to its own fingertips.

Prototypes of sports equipment clatter to the floor, hunting implements and writing tools, what look like wooden darning needles, and a descent of common or garden splinters.

What's left standing? A body block, nude of a face. You're looking down on it. Are you going to ask whether this meets a need – the feeling of falling?

How he is pitched like a tent, wide sides and thin canvas. Who manufactured the flaps, unopened and not to be opened, pre-sewn into bedrock by means he would have liked to have the power to disallow before proceeding to the same result? At a stretch my mind's eye follows its own darkness into his. Hush, hush. Tell how to hide the flatness.

Whether or not he had a spare shirt (he would have rolled it up) they might strip this one off him, hurting the buttons, unnoticed too the inequitous burn of linen momentarily interlocked with skin. And further: since neither he nor you could be relied upon to have seen lapis lazuli or ultramarine or any blue too intense to be wanted up close (the lustrous eyes of the wisdom-god Thoth the baboon, the ibis), know that this is the wrong climate for lookalikes and there are no approved markets where looks may be exchanged.

The woman with angles that from one point of view were obtuse, from another acute, showed facial signs that resembled distress in a highly developed non-expression. Much unlike a flowering tree uprooting itself – ungraciously covered with visible-grid cloth – she left her house, which was doing nothing but showing its skeleton whenever she raised her eyes, and pouring dust into the airtight jar of flour, hardly the home she had invested in. She followed somebody who had gone too far ahead, the man with the soft body, and she stopped in the door of the building that was like a lighthouse by virtue of being a building still standing in that part of town. Two other men were bullying the soft-bodied man. He was stocky, and sobbing. The shirt was now red and white: in that light, an ugly scheme. The third in the room was so much taller, and not a tormentor – doing nothing that constituted refusal, yet not taking part. The woman almost stopped breathing when she looked at that third. He was that tall, and badly jointed. That tall one stood there as if this were normal. For so long all else had been extra-normal. Her stopping scream guttered inside her when she saw the soft-bodied man turn to him whose too much quiet was enough. "You're the only one I could ever really tell how bad it's been," he sobbed in her head, and away from her hearing, and without thought of her. He hugged, and buried his face in, a chest of bones. There was kindness in the hooded inclination. For him it was at long last. The tormentors were angry and brought up short. He was out of their arms forever. The woman stayed in the doorway like a bead curtain woven to maintain a swaying chestnut and purple bird.

A whole and inhabited city that was too ancient to be convincing can, when reformatted and reconceived as ruins, continue to consist of family sites, while being more suitably picturesque than in its whole state. I saw the same owners return to picnic al fresco in what had been the living room. The space offered natural stone coffee tables and the view was now uninterrupted by what remained to suggest four walls.

This poem is for Elizabeth, who buys kebabs from the Bodrum kebab café on my new road, for Bodrum was the marvellous Halicarnassus, and Herodotus was right when he said that camels practise retromicturation (pissing through their back legs). She knows and loves him. I would believe him.

SAHARA DREAM CUBES

For Jessica Cocozza

There's much natural laughter

And some laughter left over

dream fat beauty desert indigo balance
fat dream beauty desert indigo balance
fat beauty dream desert indigo balance
fat beauty desert dream indigo balance
fat beauty desert indigo dream balance
fat beauty desert indigo balance dream

Still too thin!
Season of rains my daughter
bowls of milk   fatten when you can
sit by the lake   do not vomit
who can't walk is no cripple
you will marry a fit man

change gorgeous overnight green carpet dream
gorgeous bonebreak green carpet dream change
bonebreak steel carpet dream change gorgeous
steel tented carpet dream change stainless
tented nomadic dream change stainless dance
nomadic dream change stainless dance burial
dream change stainless dance burial rejoice

Tradition – some extenuating circumstance?
The papier-mâché dance
of those who yet can move
moves veiled and beautiful, and knows that fuller moons
draw fuller love.

Girl children force-fed in the Western Sahara

This (swelling) is (gallstones) the right (hospital) way

CALLS

For Anya K.

New past   has extra crackle pick up shell kind
where sand   pulls jokes on lovers' legs the safe kind
as hand in hand   they run down dunes the mined kind
just fast   and fortunate enough the aisled kind.

Who traced   my schoolfriend's husband's head, the slashed kind?
Who, paid,   took colour from the fields, the cane kind?
Who'd stayed   a girl in blue and white, the kind kind,
now raced   catastrophe, and not the far kind.

It needs   no patience from us. We're the heard kind.
It sends   round lots of love to all, the meant kind.
Its task   is over then, the ties of blood kind.

So end   with lots of love again the all kind.
Speed   irresponsive through the how-are-things kind.
Go ask   for natural causes where's no mind kind.

AS IN THE SUNLIGHT AND GIVEN HUMAN FORM IT IS LESS USUALLY IMPOSSIBLE TO BE SUBJECT TO THE MINUTIÆ OF WARMTH

I'd think it must be after death
                                                                  that place
if I were born to think so –
                                                                  where we'd meet
and walk towards each other
face to face
surveying without fear
              (Feel how the street has emptied,
                                                                  now you're near).
Happiness would be your name.
              (No it has not).

TEMPERATURE CONTROLLED ENVIRONMENT

You have given me a statue and I intend to keep it –
weeping as it does its miraculous unphotographed tears,
bringing to bear on the one downstairs room (not thirty paces
by thirty) outsize non-awareness who could help turning to.

I did the things for it that people do for statues:
pink net,
set sweetness –
not incense only and spangles –
fruit, camphor, wood;
blood, eventually –
to feed it and fire together dripping,
tripping various alarms I then disabled,
setting up (with settling smoke)
a lively smell of sacrifice
and singeing
the thing's skirts,
I sang out against myself,
stripped it bare.
Now it towers, how alpine, again!

Someone else might send it in procession,
blessing the streets for once with more than pedestrian shudders.

I wouldn't. It's mine, and much too heavy.

The alternative?

It is seven feet of upswept stone that makes movement awkward,
talk too, tangential, hoovering, base
stubbed soon as lit,
talk slides.
Could I just provide
a temperature-controlled environment!
Or put aside
desires to work around,

not getting round it.
Am I bound to?
(Although it blocks the galley kitchen's entrance.)
Continuous with centuries of sympathetic starving,
whenever I miss meals, I feel historical.

And I please
your statue,
that, giving no reasons,
does more to justify;
bests every suggestion by being there,
being not petty,
pretty to dust.

And the alternative?

Run yelling tensed to loosening, limbs making demonstration
stationing nowhere, hooved in mud that does not spurt, and could I
could I fix to a tilt of ninety degrees as if headlong
pedestalled never again, as if jetting into the heart
and straight into it of the sun were possible, and the sun
stands unrecognizable cracking behind the wool-wet grey
cool, cool, for ultraviolet spokes reach even a lightless day,
lighting their two-handed gift of scorch marks on a running fool.

GO FIGURE!

Yours is the face I'd want to kiss,
bliss in caressing zeros with
arrows in what epoch if not
this ah and oh aortic race
nought gaining over nought I guess
I'm gutted 'cause you don't exist.

FOR ADJECTIVES ARE ONE ROAD CUT INTO THE PRECIPICE BORDERING PERFECTION

For Carole Bourne-Taylor

According to the wall chart, the average
Neolithic lady
inhabited a body
the same size as me.

The esplanade had been enough.
Pleased like a Victorian
to walk until it gave way   find a stone
as smooth as flat   to sacrifice upon

I saw a sky the colour only of bluebells
the clear blue loved, reserved, only for bluebells
for imaginary equatorial cumulonimbus bluebells
– little like the actual absent weak-stemmed lilac flowers –

If you see,
we have that reading in common,
bleu céleste   celestial blue

TO A FLUTE, CONTINUOUS (AND THE PARTICULAR SWEETNESS)

For F. de Petrarca

She died, yet he wrote on, regardless,
still addressing himself to her ghost,
single-minded, sensitive, yet hardly
unselfish: he would win by saying most.
                                        (I'd think switch off)
Something like a song, it lasts forever
singing forgets that living hearts grip time
since through and through us music lifts out measure
sung loudening makes an always of a rhyme.
                                        (off, the particular sweetness)
Summer in the community: leaves' light
sails open-air bacteria, splashed teas;
see now the slow boy dancing to a flute –
who knows that that's rapture! – continuous.
                                        (the particular sweetness of thinking)
But winter's powerful imports throughout
both mind and evening make for certain doubt.
                                        (of thinking, your voice with my words)

THE SALAMANDER IS SO COLD

Drop adornments, endearments, rope in
hovering behaviour, trap
each look at its limits, stop don't
hit the roof – that's out of bounds, not reach –
I know that's where you're going.
            I'll steal
across its ridge, tonight, knock off ten tiles
(save that smash, but with the sound turned off,
a gift to local mosaic makers), nails
filed and filled with stuff that glints beneath,
open a hole from central heating into
cold.
            The salamander is so cold
it lives in fire, that's where it finds its level,
it strikes an average by a life in fire.
And how I'll blister, fixing your escape,
across my nature, if I have not planned
where burning creatures can find cold enough.

MORE SOLID FIRE

When along the road   the city opened,
god-like stuff that barely holds together,
more solid fire, furious,
aflame, takes a decision
for the sake of things less clear,
insists:
what is the matter?
I am
            still
                        you name me earth.

SINKING LIGHTWELLS

For the OED (Etymology)

The quarter-beds of garden, cordoned off
for building works, in this fine weather, draw you down
to look at what you're not supposed to:
others' light,
in its raw state of planning –
well below the corporate mass of foliage
sharp-sided earth
draws you down –
how many days does it take to fit a light tube?
Timetable the heart of it,
lift an already at-your-own-risk courtyard,
consider sunshine at the level where feet
cultivate potato-eyes beneath their heels,
cross, recross,
without a sense of shadow
cross, recross,
redistributing shadow,
disturbing workmen who have tabulated
installation processes for shafts of light?

And what about those many operatives,
those many office workers, well those people
who clock in underground – can they be trusted
to make good use of newly allocated,
all-natural mind-expander mood-lifter
no-excuses light? Might they cluster at breaktime
to draw down light, take a long drag on radiance
like cigarettes, to be sustained by sunshine –
there's something to work into the day.
But if they don't deserve,
aren't aware,
fail to avail themselves of it?
What if sunk light simply is
engineered true actual indefinable
happiness about them – a sudden lifting?
What if it simply is?

CALL IT SIMPLE: TWO EXTERIORS

I.

Coastal, maybe ghostly,
                                        outside, over there,
that's where the sea steals on,
                                        the place for eating up.

Oil shrugged over us slapped blackout rainbow.
If, in this defeathered situation,
something mantles, unimpressed –

This isn't it.
Not designated so.

Sense of our time in time's no sense,
no cache to requisition;
this hand's dyspraxic stammerings
no great catch,
no magician's pass.

Neither cancelled nor unpencilled.
No use.

II.

Call it simple. How to peel an apple.
All that was meant was something to hang on the wall.

See red   race away   from less and less there moist flesh
that so quickly discolours,
red once held protective round   that cyanide-seeded core,
red   made to demonstrate
the blade's wielder's no waste-maker,
red
   chivvied to resembling infinity,
red
   shying towards identity with ribbon
as if not meant for more than shredding.

Ever.
An evening scene of innocent intensity.

180° EEYLOPS

For Brian Catling

First time I install the cyclops
in the middle of my head.
This one ain't one of yours.
Owl cyclops. All thoughts recede
around about below
in hope of cover. Owl cyclops
established on a pole,
lens for one meaning only
metering nothing
mastering nothing
disporting nothing
night-time, could care less,
light-time, all lie-time.
On permanent high-beam – Nah.
Permaglare, more like.
Radiating amber that encrusts
with fear what so it contacts
which is whatsoever strikes it
which is
all air,
bespoke by predator.
Nothing escapes or sleeps.
Small animals don't know:
stop
or go.

WE'RE PROCEEDING, WEIGHTED FOR SWIFTNESS

Inconceivable

Birds, dried, small ones, peppering down, stiff-feathered,
they'd do as decorations (make them be for something),
hang them in a fringe on a red-letter day,
twirled along the banister of a pizza restaurant
(anything else?) (they can't get better than this) –

to put the thought –

but we can't stop for them, we're travelling much faster,
too fast to catch them, faster than their gravity,
and in a metal hood (they can't click) (send sounds bouncing back)
it's no good to stick out a charcoal arm from.
Weighted for swiftness, proceed: flat pockets, eyes averse,
we're on our flight path: no painful bundles, please.
Inconceivable some kind of idea of song in twigs.

OXIDANTS

Draw aside:

That gladness of the caged
presses iron furring
flakes from paint. That black
discloses other colour.
O: that air wears metal.

Know how blood rusts? Glitter,
unwashed jet hair three months
cloth-of-gold scraper. I do,
I do. Gladness. And that caged
come away striped.

Draw to:

AFTER THE EXPLOSION

"Nobody stoop!"
"It's all right. They're all standing up."
"They're standing around – what?"
"There's nothing on the ground."
"Nothing? They've looted it?"
"I told you there was not –
was nothing."
"I hope –
Look, a shopping bag has split."

> So there should be someone else there, there should be someone inside the circle, in the centre, picking up –

"Where are the goods? That's all?
Shoes, and tomato paste?"

> The group's calm. No-one's gone up in smoke.
> But what's lost –
>
> Somebody must have paid for it.
>   Somebody ought've stayed with it.
> Maybe they'd even made a list.
>   There might have been more than what's left.
> And if this crowd isn't the first –

"Nobody stoop! Tomato paste!
Shoes! Stop!"
"To whom does this belong?
Where is the shopping? Clean the ground!"

THE ROUND POND

The air above this village on the gradual hillside is so fine, so blue, it seems to spill out of wild eggshells never oozing with hatchlings, only a distillation shaken out like song, song that, glimpsed in ribbons, noted down, decides against this tracing of descent and with no kind of composure refills the sky till, dropping one by one under the musical downpour, villagers gasp agreement: "We shall keep time".

This agreement, perhaps, is why, around the pale and cheerful spire, there are spaces in this village, where houses might have been. But no. The built-up eyes of visitors read wrongly, turning back inwards to the built-up brain. "These are not spaces *for houses*. People here live with spaces". The eye looks out again, dim and unable to vault distances, while the furred heart clutches its walls; admiration and agoraphobia.

I was yet more foreign than such visitors. The histories of this village had been absorbed by me at long distance. I sought it out by choice.

Some of the villagers came close and spoke to me. "Where is the round pond?" I asked them. How did you know that existed, their quiet said.

A little way down the slope but within the village boundaries, there was the round pond. I had walked past it without passing it. I had to turn to see it. It was a few feet across. So very close.

"I know it's good for swimming," I said, confident in my reading. Who, if not themselves, had written their histories? A reaction moved all over the villagers' faces and arms and fluttered their garments: the uneasy laughter that none of them would utter, not wishing to contradict a visitor's compliment. "I wouldn't". "Not right now". "Not today, perhaps," said their movement. Perhaps the words, too, were muttered.

"People did swim here," I said, more pleasantly, and added, because I wasn't sure, "It must be safe". The laughter died from the villagers to such an extent that in the very clear air I wondered if they were alive at all.

I turned to the round pond. It was perfectly round and pitch black. The waters were not sluggish or unmoving. They were thick and still. The sun and clouds reflected off the surface. "I'm going in!" I shouted with false jollity and bent my knees. As I did so I forgot what I looked like, and felt like quite a different girl; I knew how she looked. I jumped into the centre of the round pond, scattering clear water. As I sank my hair floated up above me and seemed to create a pocket of air. I could breathe through my nose and mouth, for a limited time. Then straw was being stuffed into the water above my head, pushing me down further, but trapping air in an unscientific though very real cavity. I was moving down too fast. The water around me was filtering sun through blackness. I would come up coated in mud. About four or five bodylengths down I realized the solid ooze two bodylengths below, bottomless and exerting a great pull. I knew that if I reached that, there would be no coming up. I struggled and began to rise, not fast enough. Then I realized that the straw thrust down and the extra air had not been meant to help me. The air was to reassure me and get me sinking down further than I could swim back up to save myself without the aid of a new and unreachable lungful. Nonetheless I swam up, faster and faster.

I climbed out of the pond, coated in mud that seemed already to have slid off, the sun shining on me while I was unsure whether I looked like myself or that other girl. Like someone welcomed, I greeted the villagers. "You see I made it! Your pond is good for swimming!"

But half of them seemed to have melted away, and I could see the wind knocking holes through the ribs and tatters of the other half. The sun kept shining. I had returned to tell my story, but suspected that I was no longer alive.

THOUGHTS OF THE DEAD

Think of me as I was if that draws strength,
direct no words. I am the walking dead,
the rocking-horse child hand in plaster trace,
child of snakehole embracing stained glass head
out in the linen garden, pigsty walls.
Factory for incurious fishermen
at road's end notwithstanding, what you see
is not what was. Play steadily in gone
and done sunbeams, barring no pines, no planes
where he strode smiling mapping thinking.
Lakes, shadows, re-endeavoured, roll again
new ones to be re-trodden, lost in
anew by new ones. So great his efforts.
He described the longest trek. Take comfort,
can you, in this place approximating
to his description and your needs? Hating
his footsore and smiling lifetime, waiting
for strength, think: I was, and am no longer
alive.
Settle, settle, settle, be wise.

Thought to settle in the set of barracks
built less than carriage height you see
over there beyond the three I call them pools
oblong pits of red and burning sand.
Between the first pit and the barracks
there is a narrow strip for cultivation.
He who has gone would be happy with me
there I thought.

He did not move.

I say he went
of his own free will.

Inside the barracks: "Switch the lights on!

Switch the bleeding lights on!" "I got used –
living on my own – to moving around
in the dark, you see. I can't see clearly
without my lenses on, anyway." "Switch
the – " "No need to get nasty." "– bleeding lights –"
"The lights were on."

Only yesterday.

There. I thought.

VACANT POSSESSION

Now see them moving in: the couple, double-glazed,
refitted, lit up through slow markets, low seasons,
efficiently . . . except by lamplight, by lamplight
allowed only on holidays in old houses
where old fuels burn and, daubed with claw and feather,
slaughterboards, scrubbed, brought down from bloodshine to beechgrain,
stack unsplitting beside the steel racks and cleaver,
the invoices (ultimately at the hosts' cost)
that after all say Christmas . . . Well spent, the year turns.
The couple take this house unto themselves. To own . . .
And to be owned? Is it in the fixtures list?
How in the long room shadows linger; the cold spot;
the skirting-board's release of one knitting needle
downstairs, when the damp was being done. Victorian,
two previous owners, so much almost untouched, some
rediscoverable. With vacant possession . . .
A silent donkey brays in his stone pen, coal hole,
child's jail, the inevitable garden shed.
The sale is completed. Cardboard, rain-torn, reused,
the couple's faces pucker. Vacant. Possessed.

JOURNAL OF A FAIR SIZED CITY

For Marina Bartholomew

Black Coffee

Flamenco dancer – out of costume
buffalo-jowled, top heavy
as official war paintings –
looms witness (you recognize her from
the Matador Ball?) in the café
where mums swish, stop, consider if
they'll shop our neighbour for drugs.
"He's helped to ruin many young lives".

Never Mind the River

I like it where it's quiet. Like this road.
Floods don't reach. Angel Meadow flooded,
rowboats downed as if they never were,
park bench shoulders out, mere coathanger
to all new water under the bridge.
Furniture afloat in living rooms
on my old road, the owners away.
Cars floating from the side of your hill.
I wouldn't move. I wish I weren't renting.
No, no extra. That wall? The convent,
their garden does wonders for the air.

Hic Jacet

Tots snot, klaxons wail, vendors holler;
the modern fortress goes bleep-bleep. Follow
the better suits, the buttocks broader
than the briefcases; take the patent,
the published, the invisibly-archived route;
at the corridor's left turn, you
stay lower. Glass barriers peel aside,
ascent at the flip of a swipecard

revealed, reseals. Here lie eight hours
whose spear points fall driven out of use.

Lazy Saturday

Draw in your horns, snail; don't think of
eating those leaves – do you know how
heavy they are? Made of limestone.
Etched from mountain I abandoned.
Past where those other leaves like sharks
landed up, sunned to granny-lace
and skeletons and shoe-leather
while the neighbour who'd swapped islands
pegged out equatorial linens
yet – musically, distinctively –
sneezed in unblended Irish?

MY HIPPEASTRUMS AND MYSELF

I want to tell you all about my amaryllis,
their styrofoam dispatch in pinned packets over coastlines,
arrival early winter to flower soon thereafter,
but with white worm root coiffure not looking fit for soup,
unbelievable, too massive to be promising,
worse than swedes, like Europe's lost peasant vegetables
since legal standardization nameless and ungrown . . .
I do love them . . . all parts of the plant are poisonous . . .
tropical actually . . . the slowness of their progress,
scales greening, purpling, weeks on a sunny windowsill,
waking in ways indistinguishable from rotting,
distinct refusal to shoot, sudden telescoping.
How much they've grown!
You can't not like them; they're so scarlet,
and yet so plant-next-doorish, neat, showy, rewarding,
nice for holidays, not satin and embarrassing.
I do want to tell you about my amaryllis,
how upset I am that you find them unimportant . . .
Those are my scissors; please replace them on the shelf.

COMPLETELY F****D

After Montague Summers's translation of the Malleus Maleficarum.

Witches would detach penises
keep them in the seventeenth-century equivalent of
matchboxes
and feed them oats.

Look out the window:
horizon and white boats.

It's breakfast time.

OUTSIDE

thinking
the box the box the box the box the
thinking box the box the box the box the box thinking
the box the box the box the box the
thinking box the box the box the box the box thinking
the box the box the box the box the
box the box the box the box the box
thinking

THE VEGETABLES OF CONTEMPT

O urban blow-in, paver of private gardens,
scorning to husband allotments of thine own!
Attend local markets; the harvest is plenteous;
abandon the vitamins of alienation;
scrub off the sunblock compounded of wickedness;
nor show up swinging plastic bags lettered TESCO;
for thy repentance comes late, thou shalt be sized up,
yea, thy time shall be spent with rotten tomatoes,
thou shalt seek out and pay over the odds for 'em;
depart in gratitude, nor enquire after
certification of organic origin;
let men be what they eat; beans are too good for thee;
if thou thinkest the stall-holder handed and eyed
like a cardsharper, put thy hand in thy pocket,
pull out small change; thou despiser of toil and soil
deserv'st to have decaying chard palmed off on thee;
if fresh compost hide a mouldy stalk, that is less shame
than the moist and sinful idleness of legs
exercised upon car-pedals and adultery.

Through exploiting of thee, slowly the world improves,
and through thy unexpected, asked-for patience.
Know the seasons are in haste; and not on your side;
so turn thou betimes to the freezing of berries,
let the storage of carrots occupy thy days;
pay heed to the scampering of gnawing critters.
And yet, thou office slave, thy repentance comes late;
too late, thou speedy Urbanite; thou art condemned;
leave thy fruitless bargain-hunting; for all thy days
thou shalt eat of the vegetables of contempt.
And with that be contented.

BOLDFACED

A paper bag
leaned its earnestness
        (talking of sorts,
        asking: what burden?
        what's your next
        burden?)
towards an argument
        (idling,
        it boasts of bricks)
it cannot hold.

DON JUAN DE QUETZALCOATL
For Emily D.

Semi-Mexican sex god texted
Dame Exe,

"It's all up in the air again! touching down
near your manor, for half an hour, how 'bout
grabbing a burger, and a shag? get our claws
into that chocolate box, ease the cerise
beak back, reinstate raw Don Juan de Quetzal-
coatl, hey ain't it cute to be in agreement
just once once more baby (gotta multipack),
smart lady, waste not this player serenading
with the coca guitarra, let me revolve
your ms. independent corsetlike front door?
or let's meet in the parking lot, the airport,
the underpass, the market (I don't care for
your office), anywhere's the armpit of Eros,
let's raise a scabies of love in your city,
tunnel in, break out, off again, silver-tracked
(gotta plane booked): I'll stop over for half an hour?"

Dame Exe:

"(Tirra lirra la la la) ****! No."

OUR LADY OF STOKE NEWINGTON

For Susanna Edwards

Susanna: you'd notice her.
How many
leopards
work as photographers, attach fascinators to
bobble hats,
change their spots,
savage and golden, ripping into
mushrooms, sustained on
curly kale?
Susanna is
couched on red leather.
The Cat of Origins (answering to
her and only her, antedating
boyfriends)
sits milk-dipped.
They wonder aloud together if vanilla
makes her breasts bigger?
In some things this leopard is
precise, more than a century of microscopes
turning in her eyes.
So you trust her when she plunges
two fiery-coated arms into
a London bin, full-length,
unseen into
that Hades of discards,
pulls and
pulls. What
emerges? A crock, an orchid,
living, delivered by leopard, blooming intact.

THANKSGIVING THANK-YOU NOTE

For Erica Simms

Dear Erica,
who does not see the age of buildings
but rather walks among the trees of equal beauty
in planned woodland such as coexists with this city
called medieval, though the light's quality's best described
as pumpkin-coloured, well steamed, a giant Pyrex bowl
clamped upside down protecting all this valley; perhaps
thoughts and years by hundredweights make up the recipe,
but who really cares, except to be glad? Blink, it's autumn
at last, after floods of summer, the leaves off the trees,
whisking by, perfectly partnered by this Erica
who dances, steps making happy sense of streets that hadn't
guessed they could!
Thanks for the evening, and the pumpkin pie.

JOYFUL, TOWARDS A WEDDING DAY

For Erica Simms and Laurence Williams

Quietly now until the leaves descend
to hug the pot's base, and the week dies down
into the most conventional of shapes,
the diary fills summerlong, will shine,
a little thick and dancing crown of sparks
the colour of love budding for us all
above, through, in, the names of days. It walks
quietly now, as plain, as sweet, as known
as friendship is: Laurence and Erica:
time soon for lifelong bonding, drawing near.

THE NINTH DUCK IS CROSSING THE WATER

For Sunniva Grønlie

How is it she thinks?
Sunniva surrounded by tigers,
watchful queen whose new realm, the high bed,
her armchair-cliff-defying eyes guard.

How is it she thinks?
Crown? No. That's a hat. She's a builder.
Sunniva yawns: funny crocodiles.
The biggest duck has joined the sleep line.

How is it she thinks?
The ninth duck is crossing the water.
The door ajar, I sit on the floor
so as not to be taller than her.

TEJ JASPAL AND HIS TOOTH

For Tej Capildeo

Hey Tej, I'm envious, your first milk tooth's
out!
I loved losing mine, tormented them,
chawing into bronzefoil toffee, loosening
the bloody little ineffectual fangs,
popping out a corn, merciless, to see
unlikely roots drying clean, I couldn't
wait,
I craved the adult face to emerge,
grimmest grandmotherly Rajput jawline,
speakability of what-is-obeyed –
so alas now I'm old, I have the ache
that goes with never a full set, a poem
that's coming loose, I'm biting down on it,
wanting it out to pearl around a bit,
shape-of-a-poem squared off
gap
permanence –

YOU HAVE YOUR SPACE

Motherhood window.
Missed it.
Who has?
I have.
What window?
Watch it:

Fringes, flanges, a foreign airport, flitter of suitcases slung on the loop, always men's arms, excruciating, unlikely heft, unlifelike shapes, the hatch just beyond.

Yet another, stable-square, knotted and punched, wood cross wide and graceless conveying extra air to straw nothings.

Then the tumble-through one. Threads flag where a sequence of women, sealions, hurtled horizontal at heights past believing, half slicked to death. Slappers. Barking.

Finally, the alley of finery presenting stolen, collected, outdated stained glass angelling angles, inlaying glories peaches peacocks athwart iron pipes as the way in.

What about the one I took, that is, I missed?

By ordinary lights.

Less of the casement, less crown glass, less plate glass, lacking spandrels or lozenges or summerlong spectrum bubbling quietly of heaven drenching quick to the eye if only you'd swoop through this once.

No, I have not.
Now, what space I hold, you have.
Mine rose ordinary,
pre-modern, rounded,
let in the sun,
alike unlikes.

Love.

THE CARIBBEAN EDITOR IMAGINES EARTHQUAKES

All day Laughlin's imagining earthquakes.

> Like it's accusing itself of something,
> the house starts to pelt itself from inside:
> books like bricks, hairbrush like maracas
> rattle – rocking its occupants. Something grave.

The editor's seismically obsessed:

> At the birds' warning, the dogs' misery,
> light's flit: as from greyish to yellow: difference,
> suddenly less interrelated hills,
> the almost skittish infrasonic groan,

He's preoccupied with terremotos –

> saman trees: amber intestines steaming,
> saurian bark like a latticed piecrust, split –
> huger than the houses they're unsafe as,
> a civilization of termites spilt.

Mr. Laughlin asks, "Keep your feet on *what* ground?"

> A hospital mistake: trusting asphalt –
> the road worst taken, parting like a cut
> unhealed under its dressing – walls slabbing.
> Magma will out. Clingy geckos get thrown.

But who is he to imagine earthquakes?

> Laughlin's the man who rescues keskidees,
> securing the yellow and black fledgling,
> Sleeping Beauty in a sweetbriar hedge
> where to wake, cry bold again: *Qu'est-ce qu'il dit?*

What's he saying? Ed., you're our minor god.
Now please get a grip on two dimensions.
Reform the printed and the shining page.

Your ascetic wrists complete the keyboard.
Your subtle hands are clasped over your ears
at the bridge between sea and sky: colours
come running at you, out of place – figures,
meanwhile, stroll, enjoyably supposing
a sunset, as if this planet supports
several daily dips beneath horizons
stained like a medical slide.

No earthquake.

It's your rearing islands, they've come crowding
your office, all at once, wanting to play.

ON NOT WRITING AS A WEST INDIAN WOMAN

For those who jumped ship and drowned because the herding of people was intolerable

If you get my drift. She –
not containing oceans,
nor a spice triangle,
won't boast that cinnamon
could launch femme announcements
over the bounding main:
set course for my rich shores.
No allure for sailors.
Blackout drapes in her home.

If you stick with me. She –
hasn't cooked cassava,
nor become a mother;
might gatecrash Carnival
flaunting last year's costume
and fall down in the dance;
rack up a huge phone bill
louder than a toucan,
vexed and still calling home.

She push the boat out. She –
on a far-flung causeway
prisoners handbuilt, ice-clawed,
take her pants down, rime-clawed
over sunken warcraft,
pissing into the wind?

Birthcries repeatedly
new, self pull out self, self
issuing that self home.

AMONG

For Sveinn Haraldsson

"Liquid plus liquid
and more than liquid
a kind of safety."
This was after an attack:
winged things disliked us.
    "Here, do not tremble.
    Stem and basin, head and neck,
    keep them above this – "
"A sea from ice caps!
We could sustain nerve damage,"
    "Do you expect medusas?"
"numbness."
    "Keep moving."
A slug of crystal,
it's priming our surroundings.
I think it trembles.
Smartening, slacking,
and more than liquid liquid
mercurial.
"I can't – "
It is transparent
transparent and venomous.
But who can grasp that?

OBJECTION POETRY

Mud while the Sun Shines

For every book I read   I write an answer
Objection Poetry   poem as addenda
the museum of the Not-only-but-also
the Wonder-why-not   primarily the wonder

For this you need the adjectives   my friend said
beyond red is red and red is beyond red

I think I may not have stockpiled enough blue

Dead men row the skies in their dead men's canoe

That-something's-missing-but-not-what-is-missing
Where-shall-we-be   Where-were-we-in-all-this

The stainless the strident the desolate crew
lean down pick up publish the soul whose song fits

So who does inhabit the   Marginalia?
That's sounding rude   see I have no agenda
Objection Poetry makes mud while the sun shines
rest assured   it leaves out the Name-of-the-author

To Dance a Day-Opener

Instructions for making a J'Ouvert costume. Take several realms of oldspaper. Make a fringe for your sombrero: anything annoying, cut it up. Like strips of photos. Photos of the stripped. Say since Trinidad costumes "Made in China", you're trying to put yourself in the picture. Long gone, our creolized Muslim maker, genie of sequins from headpiece to slipper.

GROSS PIPEWORK, SUBTLE MUSIC

only dance?

say honestly   words can't dance
words can't catch the spirit
only the body   behaving badly
only the body falling about
over itself   for tragedy

trick is   thing is
only the body   can dance

the live man   they ploughed gravel over
up to his neck   he protests in favour
of green integrity   for a central Savannah
he was on the same road
as the educator   speaking for wetlands
would-be saviour   protesting for mangrove
the boat of builders   betrayed to skyscrapers
pushed him overboard

no two words about it

how much

only dance

ABOUT THE SHAPE OF THINGS

"Help me cut the world up
into paper shapes!
Then I'll know I see it.
Really.
I see it really.
Give things their names!"

> Nameless Bones Nameless Bones below oceans
> Nameless Bones we name them. That's all the names
> we have for you. The theme of everyone
> is Nameless Bones, ashamed or not to join
> in singing sea and nameless bones. Not for:
> Display. Arraignment. Arrangement. We're done.

And this morality of nameless bones
begins to stir in me against my will
to help – each flight home, every holiday,
layered by plane wings flouting nameless bones
while flickering with kinship, whispering
metal fatigue, systems' untimeliness,
the gentle letdown of oxygen masks,
profound and pressured sunless corals,
indifferent to excess of history –
against my will to help the namer. "Why
I love the radiance that names bring, arrayed
corolla-like – " "Does it need signalling,
the central secret of each thing?" "But yes,
as every secret we rejoice in. Say – "

Guyana's poet,
Martin Carter, said it:
Till I collect my scattered skeleton...

ABOUT THE BRIGHTNESS OF THINGS

I came prepared to be a shadow:

What d'you think you're up to? Tendering
your hand, which obviously is a
glove? – lady into falcon?
I'm for it – lo, stooping to the lure –

THE SERENITY

To have my head fill up with leaf forms and with light
so I can look at you with open eyes and smile
while you enjoy yourself asking the painful things,
I picture windows. A flight of words. Words in flight.

Try to penetrate my eyes. You're sent outside.
No personality sits in there; effortless,
a second nature blows you outwards. I've escaped
meantime perhaps forever slightly chill of course.

BREATHE AGAIN

For the OED (Etymology)

So it is called sternum – the breastbone?
Do you hear stern: severe: in that word?
Stern: part of a seagoing vessel
I hear, steer, starry, veridical,
without a cast back glance for white foam,
the many corrections, word history
otherwise a passion.
                                        But not when
bells, to my startlement, announcing
there exists a city innermost
harboured about the breastbone, minute
bells thrilling, the people all in joy,
heretofore unknown, hitherto mute,
launch bronze from towers' high-held glove, ringing –
an exclamation point.
                                        But silence.
How has so much gone unsuspected?
I must have been undersea: below
the wake – tailing, sunk by, my own craft?
Is this coming up too fast, bubbling
unusable oxygen in blood,
a bad case of the bends? Who'll trouble
themselves with saving?
                                        I breathe again.

VOWEL POEM: ALBEDO

Will you tell me a word
so beautiful that mourning
yields up its you to lift
an *o* towards an *r*,
or is a vowel's ghost
so powerful that mo~~u~~rning
invests with amethyst
the lily fields of dawn?
Will you tell me a word
so beautiful that morning
reflects off it – a gift –
Fearless, aurorean –

ACKNOWLEDGMENTS

'The Pale Beast' is modelled on a song that survives in France and Canada, *La Blanche Biche.*

I am grateful to the editors and compilers of *Agenda*, *Almost Island* http://almostisland.com, *The Caribbean Review of Books* http://www.caribbeanreviewofbooks.com, *The Oxford Magazine*, *Poetry Salzburg Review*, *Stand*, *Tears in the Fence*, *Archive of the Now* http://www.archiveofthenow.org, *Dusie: A Dusie Isles Reader* http://www.dusie.org/issuesix.html, and *Poetry International Web* http://uk.poetryinternationalweb.org

Thanks to: Carole Rodier Bourne-Taylor, Leila Capildeo, Brian Catling, Emma Dillon, Siân, Sunniva, and Benji Grønlie and i.m. Sverre Grønlie, Elizabeth Irwin, Sharmistha Mohanty, Rod Mengham, David Miller, Vivek Narayanan, Jeremy Noel-Tod, the Oxford English Dictionary Etymology Group, the Oxford Improvisers (especially Malcolm Atkins, Miles Doubleday and Dominic Lash) for performing and setting selections, Ron Paste, Deana Rankin, Nikki Santilli, Sarah Simblet, John Whale, Wes Williams.

This book is for Nicholas Laughlin.